Medieval Times

England in the Middle Ages

Joanne Mattern

Publishing Credits

Dona Herweck Rice, *Editor-in-Chief*
Lee Aucoin, *Creative Director*
Torrey Maloof, *Editor*
Neri Garcia, *Senior Designer*
Stephanie Reid, *Photo Researcher*
Rachelle Cracchiolo, M.S.Ed., *Publisher*

Image Credits

cover (left) The Granger Collection, (back) Bridgeman Art Library; p.1 The Granger Collection; p.4 Bridgeman Art Library; p.5 Bridgeman Art Library; p.6 Bridgeman Art Library; p.7 (top) Robert Estall photo agency/Alamy, p.7 (bottom) Shutterstock, Inc.; p.8 Mary Evans Picture Library/ Alamy; p.9 (top) The Granger Collection, p.9 (bottom) Bridgeman Art Library; p.10 The Granger Collection; p.11 (left) The Granger Collection, p.11 (right) Shutterstock, Inc.; p.12 (top) North Wind Picture Archives, p.12 (bottom) North Wind Picture Archives; p.13 Bridgeman Art Library; p.14 (left) Shutterstock, Inc., p.14 (right) Bridgeman Art Library; p.15 The Granger Collection; p.17 (top) Bridgeman Art Library, p.17 (bottom) The Granger Collection; p.18 Bridgeman Art Library; p.19 (left) Bridgeman Art Library, p.19 (right) Shutterstock, Inc.; p.20-21 Heritage Images/ Corbis; p.21 Public Domain; p.22 The Granger Collection; p.23 The Granger Collection; p.24 Bridgeman Art Library; p.25 Bridgeman Art Library; p.26 Bridgeman Art Library; p.27 (top) Library of Congress, p.27 (bottom) Bridgeman Art Library; p.28 Bridgeman Art Library; p.28-29 Bridgeman Art Library; p.32 Bridgeman Art Library; back cover Bridgeman Art Library

---

Teacher Created Materials
5301 Oceanus Drive
Huntington Beach, CA 92649-1030
http://www.tcmpub.com

ISBN 978-1-4333-5005-4

Printed by: 590835
Printed in: China

Table of Contents

A Mighty Nation

England is not a large country. It is an island on the western end of the second-smallest continent in the world. England may be a small country, but it has had a huge impact on the world.

Over the centuries, England has been ruled by several different groups. Ancient tribes were the first people to settle there. Then came people from Rome and other parts of Europe. All these different cultures shaped England into the land it is today. However, not all of these cultures met peacefully. England's history is full of adventure, battles, and plenty of drama and excitement.

England battles France in the Hundred Years' War.

Medieval London

By the Middle Ages, England was one of the most important powers in Europe. The country was a center of **commerce** (KOM-ers), learning, and the arts. Some of the most important figures in **literature** came from England. This small nation shaped the culture of many parts of the world. There is a lot of history in this little island! This land of fields, forests, and cities had its start in ancient times, but its **medieval** (mid-EE-vuhl) history started with some surprise visitors from the east.

What Are the Middle Ages?

The Middle Ages were a period in history that lasted from about 500 to 1450. This period occurred after the fall of the Roman **Empire** and before a period called the **Renaissance** (reh-nuh-SAWNTS). The Middle Ages are also called the *medieval period*. There was a great deal of unrest and change in England and other parts of Europe during this time.

England or Britain?

England was called Britain during the early years of its history. Later, England became one part of a nation called Great Britain. The other countries in Great Britain are Scotland, Northern Ireland, and Wales.

The Early Middle Ages

Invaders from the South

The Roman Empire was the most powerful empire in the ancient world. The empire began in the city of Rome. Over the centuries, the empire grew stronger and larger. Romans invaded other areas until the empire covered most of Western Europe.

The Romans leave Britain.

Some Roman roads still exist in England today.

In AD 43, Roman armies took control of the island in the western part of Europe. They named the island Britannia, or Britain. Britain became a part of Rome. A governor, sent by the Roman emperor, ruled Britain. The Romans brought many improvements to Britain. These improvements included new roads and cities.

Rome remained powerful until around the year 400. At that time, other tribes rose against the empire. There was also fighting among the Romans themselves. The Roman Empire became weak. It could no longer control so much territory. So the Romans left Britain for good.

The Romans leaving was a big shock to the people living there. The country had been ruled by the Romans for more than 350 years. The people thought of themselves as Romans and took all their orders from Rome. Now they were on their own.

Remains of the Romans

The Romans brought many changes to Britain that still exist today. The cities of London, Lincoln, and York were all founded by the Romans. Many major roads in England still follow the paths of the roads the Romans built more than 1,500 years ago.

Britain's Other People

The Romans were not the first people to live in England. Before they arrived, ancient people called **Celts** (kelts) lived in England. There were many different Celtic tribes. Britain did not have one united government until the Romans arrived.

Celtic cross

Britannia Becomes England

After the Romans left, tribes from northern Europe invaded the island. They left home in search of more land and riches. They wanted more opportunities for a better life.

Most of the new arrivals belonged to three **Germanic** tribes. These tribes were the Angles, the Saxons, and the Jutes. Over the years, the three tribes became one. The people created a new culture and language. This culture was called Anglo-Saxon. Britannia was now known as England.

an Anglo-Saxon chief

Viking ship

At first, England was divided into many small kingdoms. Over time, these kingdoms combined. Sometimes, two kingdoms united because of a marriage. Other times, a king attacked a neighbor's kingdom and took it for his own. By the late 600s, England was made up of three large kingdoms. These kingdoms were Northumbria, Mercia (MUR-shee-uh), and Wessex (WES-iks).

In the late 700s, the Vikings invaded England. They raided villages, burned houses, and stole treasure. The Vikings took control of the northeastern part of England, called the Danelaw. By 896, the Vikings had been chased out of England, but their influence remained part of English culture.

Beowulf

Beowulf (BEY-uh-woolf) is an **epic** poem that was written between the eighth and eleventh centuries. It is considered the greatest work of Anglo-Saxon literature. In the poem, the hero, Beowulf, battles two monsters that are attacking an Anglo-Saxon kingdom. He defeats the monsters and becomes king. Later, Beowulf is killed while fighting a dragon.

King Alfred the Great

Alfred the Great lived from 849 to 899. He was King of Wessex from 871 until the day he died. Alfred was the only king powerful enough to defeat the Vikings. He is also known for improving England's **legal** system. Alfred is the only English ruler who is called "the Great."

King Alfred

William the Conqueror's ship

Invaders from Normandy

In January 1066, England's king, Edward the Confessor, died. Edward did not have any children. The king's council decided that a man named Harold should be the next king. Harold was the Earl of Wessex. However, other people wanted to be king, too.

A man named William lived in Normandy, which was part of France. He claimed that he was supposed to be king after Edward died. After Harold became king, William got very angry. He and his army invaded England.

Harold had other problems besides William. In late September, his brother Tostig (TAH-stig) and the king of Norway attacked Northern England. Harold and his army went north to fight them. They hiked 187 miles (300 km) in four days! Harold defeated Tostig and his allies on September 25. Then, he heard that William was invading. Harold and his army immediately headed south to face this new problem.

Harold and William met in battle on October 14, 1066. The event was called the Battle of Hastings. Harold was killed during the battle. William declared that he was the new king of England. From then on, he was called William the **Conqueror** (KONG-ker-er). Now England was under Norman rule.

the crowning of William the Conqueror

Promises, Promises

In 1064, Harold was shipwrecked off the coast of Normandy, France. William held him prisoner but finally let him go. During this time, William said that Harold had promised him the throne of England. Harold told a different story. He said that William had forced him to promise the throne in exchange for his freedom.

The Bayeux Tapestry

The events of 1066 are recorded in thread in the Bayeux (bahy-YOO) Tapestry. This tapestry was probably stitched in England during the 1070s. It shows the events leading up to the Battle of Hastings, as well as the battle itself.

William the Conqueror

Serfs work in a field outside a walled town and castle.

How to Become a Noble

Noble titles were usually passed down from father to the oldest son. Younger sons might have lesser titles and smaller pieces of land. Someone could also become a noble if he did something important for the king. Then the king might grant that person a title and land to go with it.

The Code of Chivalry

Knights had an important job. They were warriors who defended the king and their lords. Knights also followed a strict code of honor. This code was called ***chivalry*** (SHIV-uhl-ree). Chivalry demanded that knights be polite, respectful, brave, loyal, and helpful to those in need.

A man is knighted.

A Feudal Society

Medieval English society was very organized. It was a **feudal** (FYOOD-l) society. In a feudal society, a person's position depended on how much land he had. Feudalism brought order to society and allowed most people to work and provide for themselves. However, it was a harsh system.

The king was the most important person in a feudal society. Under him were nobles. Nobles were loyal to the king. In exchange for their loyalty, the king gave nobles large amounts of land. The nobles used this land for farming and raising animals. A noble could earn a lot of money from the land he controlled.

Serfs farm the land.

Below the nobles were vassals (VAS-uhlz). Vassals were usually knights and soldiers. They protected the king. Under the vassals were serfs. Nobles did not farm the land themselves; serfs did.

Serfs, also called ***peasants***, had only a small piece of land to call their own. Almost everything else belonged to the nobles above them. In return, the serfs had a place to live and protection from danger. Serfs had few rights and had to obey the nobles. The serf was similar to a slave, except that the serf could not be sold to another noble.

Important People of the Middle Ages

Many fascinating people lived in England during the 1100s. Here are just a few of them.

King Henry II

Henry II

King Henry II ruled England from 1154 to 1189. He was the great-grandson of William the Conqueror. In some ways, Henry was a great king. He changed England's legal system and introduced jury trials. Jury trials resulted in a more just system. However, Henry also had a very bad temper. He often fought with others.

Becket's murder

Thomas Becket

Thomas Becket was an archbishop. When Henry tried to take some of the Church's power away, he and Thomas became bitter enemies. To please Henry, four knights murdered Becket in Canterbury **Cathedral** in 1170. In 1173, Thomas was declared a saint by the church.

Eleanor of Aquitaine

Eleanor of Aquitaine

Eleanor of Aquitaine (AK-wi-teyn) was Henry's wife. Eleanor was one of the wealthiest and most powerful women in Europe. She and Henry had eight children. Two of their sons would become kings of England. However, Eleanor and several of her sons **rebelled** against Henry's rule. To punish her, Henry put Eleanor in prison for 16 years.

Three Kings in One Family

Henry II ruled England, but he could not rule his own family. His sons rebelled against him. They fought over Henry's French lands as well as who would become king of England. Richard was Henry's oldest surviving son. He finally became king when Henry died. Since Richard I did not have any children, his brother John I succeeded him on the throne.

England's Queen

Eleanor won her freedom when her son Richard I came to the throne. Richard spent many years away from England fighting wars called the Crusades. During his absence, Eleanor ruled England as the unofficial queen.

A Lion Fights

Richard I became king of England in 1189, but he was more interested in events away from home. At that time, many soldiers were fighting in religious wars called the Crusades. The Crusades tried to restore Christian rule to the Middle East, or the Holy Land. These wars lasted from 1095 to 1291. Kings, nobles, knights, and peasants from all over Europe fought in the Crusades. In the end, however, their efforts failed.

Richard left England in 1190 and did not return until 1194. Then he went off to the Crusades again. In 1199, he was wounded in battle and died soon afterward. Richard spent only six months in England during his entire **reign**. Richard never even learned to speak English. Instead, he spoke French.

Richard may not have been the best king, but he was very popular with the English people. He received the nickname "the Lion Heart" because he was so courageous. Richard was also handsome and charming. He was the subject of many adventure stories and songs. He is still a popular figure today and remains one of England's most famous kings.

King Richard I

Captured!

King Richard I was traveling back from the Holy Land in 1192 when he was captured and held prisoner by Emperor Henry VI of Germany. Richard's mother, Eleanor of Aquitaine, paid a **ransom** and won his freedom two years later.

The Legend of Robin Hood

Robin Hood is one of England's most famous heroes. He was an **outlaw** who lived in Sherwood (SHUR-wood) Forest. Robin and his men robbed rich travelers and then gave the money to the poor. They were loyal to King Richard and fought with him in the Crusades. Robin Hood may have been based on a real person, but no one knows for sure.

Robin Hood

The Lords Strike Back

After King Richard I died, his brother John I became king of England. While Richard was popular, no one cared for John. He was a weak king who was neither respected nor liked. He had even plotted to take over the throne while Richard was still alive. The nobles finally had enough of the weak king. They banded together, created an army, and went after John in London.

The lords forced John to sign a document in 1215. This paper was called the Magna Carta (MAG-nuh KAHR-tuh), or the Great Charter. The Magna Carta spelled out some new rules. It said that the king had to obey the laws. It also said that he could not collect taxes or pass new laws without the lords' permission. If the king broke a law, the lords could kick him out and choose a new king.

King John I signs the Magna Carta.

the Magna Carta

John hated this document, but he knew he had to sign it. The Magna Carta is one of the most important documents in history. It paved the way for other documents that explained how leaders should rule. In England, it set the stage for a strong **Parliament** (PAHR-luh-muhnt) and became the basis for the people's rights.

The Birth of Parliament

The first official Parliament met in 1272. Parliament made suggestions that the king had to follow. After 1327, Parliament was divided into three parts: the king, Lords, and Commons. The House of Lords included noblemen and religious leaders. The House of Commons included knights and business leaders.

False Promises

King John I had no intention of following the rules in the Magna Carta. His actions led to a war with the lords. When John died in October of 1216, the lords supported his young son, who became King Henry III.

Henry III

A War, a Plague, and a Revolt

The Hundred Years' War

During the Middle Ages, England's kings often came from France. This was because of the close ties between England and Normandy. France had its own king, and he did not like that England controlled so much land in his country. This conflict led to a very long war.

The Hundred Years' War actually lasted for more than 100 years. In 1337, King Philip VI of France tried to take English land in southwestern France. England fought back, and a series of battles followed.

Battles were now different from how they had been in the past. **Archers** became more important than fighting men on horseback. The most useful weapon in this war was the **longbow**, which could shoot an arrow over a greater distance and do more harm to the enemy. Knights' armor had also been improved. It was now stronger and jointed. This allowed the knights to move their arms and legs.

There were many battles during the course of the war. In 1453, the French drove the last of the English armies out of France. Finally, the Hundred Years' War ended.

The French battle the English during the Hundred Years' War.

Geoffrey Chaucer

A Famous Prisoner

One of England's most famous writers had an interesting role in the Hundred Years' War. On March 1, 1360, young Geoffrey Chaucer (CHAW-ser) was running an errand for the king's forces. Chaucer was captured by a group of French knights and held prisoner by their lord. The French lord quickly discovered that Chaucer was a servant to the **royal** family. King Edward III paid a ransom to free him.

Chaucer would go on to write *The Canterbury Tales*. This long poem is a collection of stories told by travelers on the way to Thomas Becket's shrine in Canterbury. It is one of the most famous works in English literature.

A Horrible Death

Around 1348, a disease called the ***bubonic plague*** (byoo-BON-ik playg) struck England and most of Europe. Many called it the Black Death. The Black Death was carried by fleas that bit humans and spread the sickness. The Black Death was a horrible disease, and its victims usually died within a few days. The disease spread quickly, completely wiping out entire towns and villages.

The Black Death spread rapidly because people lived so close together. Crowded streets and buildings were full of rats, which carried fleas. The filthy conditions allowed the germs to spread even faster. The Black Death killed more than 1.5 million people between 1348 and 1350.

The Black Death strikes England.

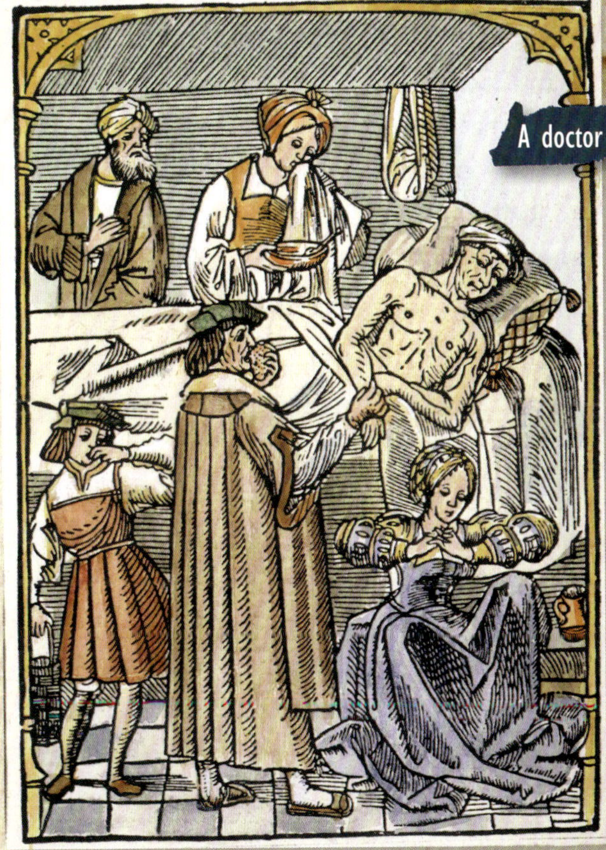

A doctor visits a plague victim.

The Black Death changed English society. So many men had died that there were not enough workers to farm the **estates**. That meant there was a higher demand for laborers. Peasants left their fields to find better jobs. They also asked for better pay. This made the lords angry, so they tried to stop the peasants from moving or demanding more money. However, the peasants did not go down without a fight.

The Spread of the Plague

The Black Death started in China and spread to Europe on **merchant** ships. These ships were always filled with rats and fleas. There were six major outbreaks of the plague in Europe during the 1300s. The disease did not disappear until the 1600s.

A New Law

To stop peasants from wandering around the countryside asking for better pay, the government passed a law in 1351. This law said no one could pay wages that were higher than the wages paid in 1346. It also said workers had to stay in their own villages.

The Peasants' Revolt

Society changed after the Black Death. The peasants demanded more freedom and better pay. However, the lords denied their requests. The peasants became even angrier when the government demanded that they pay a poll tax. This tax was to help pay for England's war with France.

In June 1381, the peasants decided to **revolt**. A group of peasants marched from Essex (ES-iks) into London. Their leader was a man named Wat Tyler. This Peasants' Revolt is also called Wat Tyler's Rebellion.

Wat Tyler leads the rebellion.

When the peasants arrived in London, King Richard II met with them. He agreed to all of their demands. The king then asked them to go home peacefully. But some of the peasants stayed and killed the archbishop of London and the king's treasurer.

Richard and London's mayor met with the **rebels** again outside the city. The mayor and some of the king's men killed Tyler. The peasants went back home. After they left, the king refused to keep any of the promises he had made, except for getting rid of the poll tax.

King Richard II meets with the rebels.

A Sad End for All

Wat Tyler was not the only leader of the Peasants' Revolt. Jack Straw and Father John Ball also helped Tyler. Like Tyler, Straw and Ball were killed by the king's men. Their bodies were displayed in London to scare people so they would not rebel again.

A Young King

Richard II was only 10 years old when he took the throne and became king. He was only 14 years old when he faced the rebels outside London. Because he was so young, the king had a group of men who counseled him and helped him make decisions.

War of the Roses

Many people wanted to be king of England, and it was not always clear who had the best claim to the crown. King Richard II was the grandson of Edward III. However, Richard II's cousin, Henry IV, thought he should be king. In 1399, Henry defeated Richard and claimed the crown.

Richard II and Henry IV

Henry IV and his **heirs** ruled until the 1450s. Then another Richard, the Duke of York, decided he had the right to the throne. His reason was that he was **descended** from Edward III. Some noble families sided with the Duke of York. Others sided with Henry VI of the House of Lancaster. The two sides fought a war called the War of the Roses.

The first battle was fought at Saint Albans (AWL-buhnz) in 1455. The two sides continued to fight off and on, with the crown going back and forth between the two families.

In 1485, Henry Tudor (TOO-der) defeated King Richard III at the Battle of Bosworth. The Lancastrians had finally won the war, and Henry became King Henry VII. He married a daughter of one of the Yorks, which united both houses and ended the war.

King Richard III

William Shakespeare

The War of the Roses in Literature

More than a hundred years after the War of the Roses ended, the famous English writer William Shakespeare wrote about it. Shakespeare wrote several historical plays that described the war and the kings who fought in it, including Richard II, Henry IV, Henry V, Henry VI, and Richard III.

Red and White

This conflict was called the War of the Roses because each side had a rose as its symbol. The Yorks used a white rose. The Lancastrians used a red rose.

The End of the Middle Ages

King Henry VII was a very clever man. He faced many threats when he came to the throne. One of his first acts was to build a strong royal army. Before that, the king depended on the lords and their armies to fight for him. Henry wanted an army that was only under his command.

Henry knew that a rich king was a strong king. He raised a lot of money by taxing the lords. This also kept the lords from having too much power. Henry also promoted good relations with other countries. He married his son to a Spanish princess to make sure Spain would be England's friend.

King Henry VII

When Henry died in 1509, England was a powerful country. The nation had changed a lot over the centuries. England had been part of Rome and then a nation ruled by different tribes. England had faced years of warfare and struggles between the rich and the poor. The Middle Ages were now over, and England was entering a new period called the Renaissance. During this time, England would become even more powerful.

Oxford University

Centers of Learning

In the early Middle Ages, the sons of noble families studied with private teachers. By 1500, they were able to study in several universities. The most important universities in England were Oxford and Cambridge.

Oxford University was founded in the city of Oxford in the late 1100s. It was England's first university. By 1209, there were around 1,000 students at Oxford. That same year, some students left Oxford to study at another university called Cambridge.

Cambridge was started by a bishop. At first, the school only had a handful of students. All of the students there had to study religion. But they also studied other subjects, such as Latin, mathematics, and science.

Glossary

archbishop—the highest ranking Catholic bishop within a region

archers—people who fight using a longbow

bubonic plague—a serious and often deadly disease carried by fleas from infected rats

cathedral—a large and important church

Celts—people who lived in Britain in ancient times

chivalry—a code of behavior expected of a knight

commerce—the buying and selling of goods and services

conqueror—someone who defeats another country

descended—part of a later generation of the same family

empire—a group of countries that has the same ruler

epic—long and important

estates—large areas of land

feudal—having to do with a government where people worked and fought for a lord in return for protection

Germanic—a group of tribes from early Europe

heirs—people who inherit or have the right to inherit property

legal—having to do with laws

literature—written works that have lasting value or interest

longbow—a large bow that shoots arrows

medieval—the Middle Ages

merchant—a person who buys and sells goods for profit

outlaw—someone who has committed a crime and is running away from the law

Parliament—a governing body in the United Kingdom

peasants—people who worked on farms during the Middle Ages

ransom—money paid to free someone from captivity

rebelled—fought against a person or the government

rebels—people who fight against the government

reign—a period of time when a ruler is in power

Renaissance—a period of time in which European culture experienced a revival of art, science, and literature

revolt—to rise up against a power

royal—having to do with kings and queens

Index

Your Turn!

In 1215, the lords forced King John I to sign the Magna Carta. The Magna Carta said that the king had to obey the laws, too. If the king broke the laws, the lords could choose a new king.

Medieval Poetry

Study the painting and think about what you learned about the Magna Carta. You will write an acrostic poem about the important document. Write the words *Magna Carta* vertically down the middle of a piece of lined paper with one letter on each line. Then, for each letter, come up with a word or phrase that describes the document and also begins or ends with one of the letters in *Magna Carta*.